www.finishinglinepress.com

Flow Variations

poems by

Andrew C. Gottlieb

Finishing Line Press
Georgetown, Kentucky

Flow Variations

ACKNOWLEDGMENTS

Individual Publications

Best New Poets 2013: "Portrait: Parsing My Wife As Lookout Creek"
Briar Cliff Review: "Submerged"
The Flyfish Journal: "Ode to Smith Meadow"
saltfront: "Considering a River: Lookout Creek, Writing, and a Brief Meditation
on Flow"

Publisher: Leah Maines

Editor: Christen Kincaid

Cover Art: Ericka Wolf

Author Photo: Jenny C. Fan

Cover Design: Elizabeth Maines

Printed in the USA on acid-free paper.
Order online: www.finishinglinepress.com
also available on amazon.com

Author inquiries and mail orders:
Finishing Line Press
P. O. Box 1626
Georgetown, Kentucky 40324
U. S. A.

Table of Contents

For everyone working to conserve, preserve, and protect clean water

I'm taking a water walk, hiking down the intermittent streamlets (on this summer day they are just damp fingerings) that converge somewhere in here to set the river off on its ocean course...

—William Least Heat-Moon, *PrairyErth*

Ode to Smith Meadow

I miss Fish Creek,
meadow stream
waist-thin, bent
again under shaggy
banks, slanting grass,
hanging weed
and alpine flower,
swale-placed stream
with a headwater
chill, chiseled
pasture channel
canyon-bound, down-
ward tending, slope
only slight at Sierra
heights, angling
as gravity asks,
pooled in places
sheltering trout,
showy goldens,
fingerlings, larger
fish, elders that winter
over, lingering,
invisible, then leaving
rings, rippled
dimples, sipping
surface bugs under,
midges, nymphs
close to the wing,
hatches of rapid
miniatures filling
the low sky, cattle-
high, drifting pollen-
like over the scene,
Fish Creek, Smith
Meadow, acrobatic

swallows, the herd,
slumbering,
what sways in me
in that place, all
of us grazing
the gift of the
recumbent day.

Landscape: North of Pavilion Key

When the wind dies over the low tide, it's a hot desert on the slack flats.
The sea trout hold in the eel grass below,
but the day's only bite is the slap of the sun's reprimand
coming off the water, singeing your face steady red
under a limp-brimmed hat for being out here alone, for slipping the skiff
through the keys' curves along the indistinct boundaries of distance,
angle to plane, red mangrove span to sand's gentle slope,
to land out on no land, the tender skin of such glittering difference.
The silhouette of an unnamed bird floating far starboard could be called
reason, but so can the taut voices that surprise from behind
as you gaze to the gulf's horizon where nothing can be seen,
nothing's there to anchor what you hear in the sleepy heat
while you try to divine words: tern or shearwater or fishing. Beneath,
sand bars lazily wait for their next invisible shift,
and as the late blue blaze begins to relinquish its best effort,
you squint to decide between island or eye-trick,
afterimage or schooling newness, about the bleary black shapes
speckling the southernmost edge of your perception.

The Walking Gods

The weight of the descending flow—heavy, cold,
dedicated to places downstream—confronts you
while you stare alone for giant cutthroat,
mythic, in the deepest pools.

There are gods in these woods, pounding slopes
and meadows, the weight of seasoned legs
plunging spongy hole to hole.

A river never forgives, never compromises
its vision. The biggest boulders thunder
as they trundle on the bottom.

Deep in the old growth, you feel a presence,
a recent breath, the deepest scent on rocks
left traced by the navigation of mosses.

A walking stick and a steady step prevent accidental
drowning. The river's intimate tug presses
its indifferent love like a rope. Elsewhere, the tall gods
bustle. One stubborn bole leans over
like the oldest, strictest teacher.

Submerged

Below the broad dock, beneath
    the scarf of mist,
the heavy cat settles
    in the black water.

It's the quiet like this I crave,
    before the sun
stabs at everything with its
    audacious knowing.

Early mornings, my father
    sat alone,
but could not teach
    what this meant.

The thick fish offers the slightest
    tailfin ripple.
Long whiskers wander the close
    pond bottom.

What choice for small eyes
    in the dark?
To try to read the muddy, unprinted
    ribbon of night.

We already know each day brings
    its glittering assault.

Considering a River: Lookout Creek, Writing, and a Brief Meditation on Flow

I will tell you of a river, Lookout Creek. Of writing about that river.
Of ways to think about and experience that

river.

The act of writing balances experiencing the object and interpreting the object,
an exercise that is no longer the object at all,
and thus deals with symbols and interpretation
of certain perceptions.

Lookout Creek flows
through the 16,000 acre H.J. Andrews
Experimental Forest on the western side of the Willamette National Forest,
emptying out
into
Blue River Reservoir. The creek, as wide and fast as it might be, is only about 5 or 6 miles long: perhaps why it's called a creek. About an hour east of Eugene, Oregon, the Andrews Forest is a research forest, a Long Term Ecological Research site, and one of the benefits of that designation is that Lookout Creek, flowing in a research area, is closed to fishing.

A river is a linear object,

in a way, but it's impossible

    to experience it linearly.

            We experience it
non-linearly.
      A hunk here, a hunk
                there.

Even floating the course of an entire river,

              that's how   it is.

I was determined to hike all of Lookout Creek, not along the shore, on a
dirt trail, but in the water, wearing waders, walking that moving,
wet trail. From its emptying mouth at Blue River Reservoir
to its headwaters under Lookout Mountain…

...a place not linear at all,

the *Now* in writing is a difficult fast-moving place, a vibrating, uneasy, active
interpretation where the nearest of futures—a brief vision—collides, concentrates, interacts, juggles, challenges, fuses, and somehow lands, becoming concrete: a solid interpretation of the object of the past, letters and words
             in linear order on the page.

A linear order that is not the object it purports to represent that is

             already long gone...

...and is perhaps not linear.

             In the river, there's water above you,

and water below you.
              You look hard. It looks like all the same water.
But the water at your feet is always different. You can't stop it.
It's all the same, and yet there is clearly different water
above you, about to arrive,
              water at your feet, right here,
                    and water already past

you,

long gone.

Five miles doesn't sound like too long of a hike for an able-bodied walker
       on reasonable ground. Hiking five miles in a river
                          is a different story.
The pressure of calf-deep water moving at a clip adds what feels like
pounds
       of weight to your feet.

The minute I sit and start typing the letters that accumulate to words: the object
          comes, and the object is gone
as I'm watching it, the object becomes my imagination of the object,
          my interpretation of what
                              I remember the object to be.
Then I look up and again it's...

There is just one Lookout Creek, as there is just one poem, this essay.
          Yet, perhaps every reader of the essay
                    reads a different river,
                                        wades a different poem.

Perhaps there are as many Lookout Creeks as there are readers of this essay.

                                        That implies
a potentially unlimited number of Lookout Creeks and poems
in existence, creation, and interpretation.

In trying to hike all five miles of Lookout Creek, I saw a lot of the river,

but the actual distance I waded, over the course of many days,
                                                    was probably closer
to a mile.

          A hunk here.

A hunk

there.

Wading, you can feel the push of the water, the pull of the current.
You can look upstream, and see water
that has not yet reached you, and you can look below you,
and see water that has flown past you.
This coming and going of water is constant. All you can do is watch.
That is to say, you can watch all you want,
but you can't change the motion of the actual object.

Where does all that water come from? This may be a question of fact
or of impression, of real awe.

I tell you of a river,
                    Lookout Creek,
                                and you picture a river you know,

a specimen

that most approximates your idea of
                                river.
                                        I tell you how beautiful it is,
this research stream closed off to fishing, flowing vigorously
through an old growth forest, inaccessible, much of it, even to a person
wading.

Inaccessible: rocks, cutbanks, riffles, holes, pocket water, deep pools, the
turquoise and aquamarine colors of the shallows and depths revealed
in the afternoon sunlight
filtering through the tall old growth.

                        You picture your own favorite

                                            river.

There is a large rock.

I feel like sitting down on this rock—this exposed platform that has water
lapping at its sides but a dry upper surface—so I can rest,
so I can just watch the
                        (Lookout Creek)
                                        coming and going.

Though if I sit, I'm losing ground against my goal of hiking the entire five-
mile length of this challenging, deeper than expected

                        river.

The thing with writing is it always puts you one step away from the object.

Seeing and being with the river,
standing in Lookout Creek,
watching the water rush around your calves, pulling at your wading staff,
feeling the cold,
hearing the sound of the falls, pools, and eddies colliding
with and moving around strewn boulders, stones, fallen boles,
the chaos of the bale-like debris collected and pressed into piles
by the weight of the water,
stepping in and over the freestone bed of this river,
seeing the huge, vertical, live trunks of old growth Douglas firs
that border and help define the bank,
and, at the ground, the salal, the holly, the ferns,
the wet, dark green undergrowth
hanging over the moving, black water: at that point, only a fool writes.

Look,

        here is a river called Lookout Creek.

                By *look*, I mean *read*,

but ironically, look seems a far better word for the implied transaction

between writer and reader.

We read but we want to *look*.

We write but we want to *look*.

I could write that Lookout Creek stops, could tell you how I waded
        downstream
amid this rushing water—water above
        that was always coming to me,
then was passing me,
        then was below me,
water always below me,
        moving on,
the same water, it seems,
        but different,
as we've said—and I kept going downstream,
        carefully, rather than upstream,
and I came to this place in the river where the water suddenly stopped.

Stopped dead in its tracks!

There it was, the water, and I could hold it and assess it.
        However, this didn't happen
and is not in the nature of rivers.
A stopped river is something we typically refer to
        as a lake,
but even a lake usually
                                        has a certain motion to it.

Flow.

What questions are we asking?

Questions of cold feet, of impression.

Of motion and helplessness.

In the dark, at night, the hillsides of the headquarters of the
Andrews forest
look black, even darker than the sky, the contours and edges
smoothing out, disappearing, and the impression
is one of standing in a dark vessel, nature's cupped hands
cradling this collection of buildings that allow access to the forest.

A black-tailed deer grazing only a few feet away

may be invisible.

Both of you hear the river, Lookout Creek.

Fellowship

Your friend says, God, I love women, and who's to argue,
the truck bouncing up the ruts and dips
of the two-track forest path on the bumpy plunge
to the river. The mysterious way we worship
what's missing, evening dreams considering angles
of flow, cut-banks, cryptic pools of dark, holy promise,
meander scars and the driftwood mark
of a periodic flood.
                            At the edge, we split, stepping
into the shallow lap—symptom of the serious current's
further water commanding the deep channel,
force that takes breath and balance with her only nature—
ready to clamber bankside over
                                      wet boulders, low
limbs,
to reach the best eddies, but alone, we'll do it alone,
steady strive for the best heavy cutt in that volume
of cold motion,
                      line tight to the wild other,
quest that brings us together only momentarily to relish
what we hope to briefly hold, blessing for which we sacrifice
one another: the sudden silver flash of bare muscle,
thrashing length in the day's hallowed splash.

Portrait: Parsing My Wife as Lookout Creek

My wife sits, wipes, stands, zips, forgets to flush.
                                                    Rushing,
the river's every agenda. We pull at our clothing,
        all day, humans, us,
                        all of us.
                                Try not to touch it.

I stand at the mirror, tuck a tail, a tag, tug a collar, flinch.
        What face is that?
                        Dry
outside, there are pines pushing against every reflecting sky
        in their own grim time.

My mother, tough one, British stiff.   *Sit up straight. Excuse
        you. That's a dessert spoon.*
                                Butler's fool,
ambassador for a childhood of rules.   One tough one.

Language gets us in its grip with its little links and latches,
        clasps, clamps,
                        padlocks,
                                and we're lost: grappling.

Close your mouth when you chew.
                                In these river days,
what floats for me to find is the tissue, wet, a red filmy swirl
        the symptom of a drifting of cells
                                alluvial shift
in a body I know.

                        Do you imagine first the conifer leaves?
Or the buried thread-like roots
        deeply reaching for food?
                                Plunging to touch the hidden skin
        of the river.

Dawn's lazy diffusion of hues lights the children's
confusion, their breakfast food,
                   flow
                           of this river that spews
stripped trunks, a shoe, crescent crust of dead everything,
                the ongoing plunge of innard and corpse.

Even my stepdaughter laughs, who for now laughs last,
                               least.
There's nothing funny about PMS: period.
                            My wife,
sure, she blushes, but it's love like the cat's torn mouse,
   the breast-split wren,
                 the rejected owl pellet,
                          her kind of love,

the river's necessary way of sharing of what she's composed,
   unburdened by grammars, maps, latitudes, rules,
banks.
        I am wading
              the lava rock and free-stone bed,

the old-growth bole
             wedged
                   and lecturing only by collecting
every drifting thing that the muscle spits up, aggregate of flow,
   motion of bundling,
clustered abundance of the rushing's best refuse.
                         I steady my step,
pocket a bottle, sift the river with my fingers, sink
             into its stunning flood,
                 touch her every part.

Additional Acknowledgments

Thanks: to Leah Maines, Christen Kincaid, and everyone at Finishing Line Press for supporting this chapbook; for originally getting these poems into print: Brenda Shaughnessy, Jazzy Danziger, Tricia Currans-Sheehan, Steve Duda, Michael McLane, and Eric Robertson; for support that allowed some of these poems to happen: Deborah Mitchell and everyone at Artists in Residence in Everglades, Inc. (AIRIE,) and at Everglades National Park, Rick Rivero for his guidance and hospitality, and Keith Waddington for his insight to bees, botany, and brews; likewise, at the H.J. Andrews Experimental Forest and Oregon State University's Spring Creek Project: Charles Goodrich, Kathleen Dean Moore, Fred Swanson, and Kathy Keable; to all staff and scientists that keep these vital places alive and protected while helping provide access to artists and writers; to Ericka Wolf for her gorgeous painting; to Jim Edwards for getting me on my first golden trout at Rattlesnake Meadow; to Derek Sheffield for feedback, poems, and trips to Icicle Creek; to Jenny, Seb, and Maddie who can all land trout; to the rest of the poets, naturalists, fly fishers, and waders, all of you, too many to name: here's to the waters.

Born in Ontario, Canada, **Andrew C. Gottlieb** grew up outside of Boston, Massachusetts, and since 1998, he's lived on the West Coast of the United States, dividing his time between Southern California and the Pacific Northwest. He taught composition and short story writing at Iowa State University and at the University of Washington, where he received his MA and MFA in English and Creative Writing, respectively.

He's been awarded grants from the Seattle Arts Commission and the Seattle-based Artist Trust Foundation, and has been writer-in-residence at six different—often wilderness—locations including Denali National Park, Everglades National Park, the H.J. Andrews Experimental Forest, Isle Royale National Park, and the Kimmel Harding Nelson Center for the Arts.

His writing has appeared in many anthologies and journals including *American Fiction, Best New Poets, Denver Quarterly, Ecotone, The Fly Fish Journal, Mississippi Review, Orion, Poetry Northwest, Poets & Writers,* and *Tampa Review,* and he's currently on the editorial board for *Terrain.org: A Journal of the Built + Natural Environments.*

When he's not reading, writing, or with his family, he can often be found on a river.

CPSIA information can be obtained
at www.ICGtesting.com
Printed in the USA
BVOW09s1111261217
503583BV00001B/21/P